A STEGOSAU... IS FOR LIFE

AND OTHER ANIMAL POEMS

TREVOR MILLUM

ILLUSTRATIONS BY ELAINE HILL

ISBN 0-9542710-7-6

First published 2006 by Hands Up Books

For further information, please contact:
Graham Denton (editor), 1 New Spout Hill Cottages, Brantingham HU15 1QW, East Riding of Yorkshire

Printed in the UK by Central Print Services, Hull

This book is for Jacob and Joe,
and Daisy and Molly;
of course not forgetting,
Georgie and Ollie.

Contents

Spring in the Yarm Fard

The mat keowed
The mow cooed
The bog darked
The kigeon pooed

The squicken chalked
The surds bang
The kwuk dacked
The burch rells chang

And then, after all the dacking and the changing
The chalking and the banging
The darking and the pooing
The keowing and the kooing
There was a mewtiful beaumont
Of queace and pie-ate.

ssshhhh !!
Queace and Pie-ate

2

I've got a pet shoe

It sits in the corner
With its laces all neat,
It never runs off:
It'll stay by your feet.

It doesn't bark at the cat
Or scratch at the door,
Doesn't meow to be fed
Or leave pools on the floor.

It eats very little,
Well, almost nothing at all.
It'll sit on the chair
Or wait in the hall.

It likes to go walkies
Wrapped round my toes,
Keeps close to heel
Wherever I go.

Mum gets quite cross
"Get that thing off my table!"
"But mum, it's my pet -
See, it's got a pet label!"

I've called it Jemima
(A name all its own);
Hmmm, I think I might get a trainer
So it's not so alone...

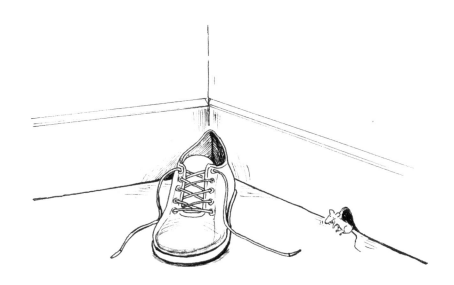

You're the Best

I love the way
You nod your head
I love the way
You walk ahead
I love the way
You sneak on my bed
I love the way
You chew the mail
I love the way
You wag your tail
You cheer me up
You never fail
Your fur's uncombed
Your coat's a mess
But I love you
And you're the best
Yes I love you
You are the BEST!

Teacher's Pet

He brought it into school last week.
It sits quite quietly, gives no cheek.
We asked him why.
He said, "Don't fret.
It's more than just a simple pet;
We have an understanding, see?

I teach him
- and he heeds me!
I need him
- and he needs me.
Puts up a paw before he talks,
is obedient when out for walks.
He likes my voice;
I like his style;
I think we'll be together for a while...
You see, when I feel I'm getting old,
when you lot won't do as you're told,
I look at Mac
he looks at me,

I think - 'He could eat you lot for tea'.
That always makes me smile
and so that's why he's here.
I knew you'd understand."

I looked at Mac,
he looked at me.
I understood all right.

Sunday

Monday

One Cat, All Cats

On Sunday, I'm Sandy the Sunday cat
Sitting on the settee where *you* sat:
Sandy, Sandy, the Sunday cat.

On Monday, I'm Mandy the Monday cat
Mewing and moaning on the mat:
Mandy, Mandy, the Monday cat.

On Tuesday, I'm Choosy, the Tuesday cat
Chasing the chaffinch - just for a chat:
Choosy, Choosy, the Tuesday cat.

On Wednesday, I'm Wendy, the Wednesday cat
Watching the rain go pit-a-pat:
Wendy, Wendy, the Wednesday cat.

Tuesday

Wednesday

Thursday

On Thursday, I'm Thirsty, the Thursday cat
Furry and fluffy and thoroughly fat:
Thirsty, Thirsty, the Thursday cat.

On Friday, I'm Freddy, the Friday cat
With friendly fleas from next-door's flat:
Freddy, Freddy, the Friday cat.

Friday

On Saturday, I'm Sooty, the Saturday cat
Sitting slyly on your special hat:
Sooty, Sooty, the Saturday cat.

Whatever day of the week you choose
I'm there beside you. You can't refuse!
Monday to Sunday and in between
I'm the best cat you've ever seen.

Saturday

Hippo, hippo

Hippo, hippo
Where have you been?
I've been to the swamp;
I hid in the stream.

Hippo, hippo
What did you see?
I saw all the rushes
And reeds around me.

Hippo, hippo
What will you do?
I'll lie with my mouth open
Waiting for you!

Poor Claudius the Croc

A crocodile called Claudius lived by a big wide river.
This crocodile called Claudius made other creatures shiver.
His snout was long, his teeth were sharp, his eyes were steely grey;
As soon as you caught sight of him you'd surely run away,
(A pity: all he wanted was for you to stay and play).

Sometimes a visitor would come and look at lonely Claude
Where he was lying on the mud, alone and feeling bored;
And Claude would sniff and snuff, and open up an eye
And as a kind of welcome his smile would open wide.
(How sad he was when visitors ran away to hide!)

So dear readers of these lines, wherever you may be,
Do not make up your minds just on what you see.
Like Claudius, our outsides may give a wrong impression
So look beneath the surface - a very useful lesson!

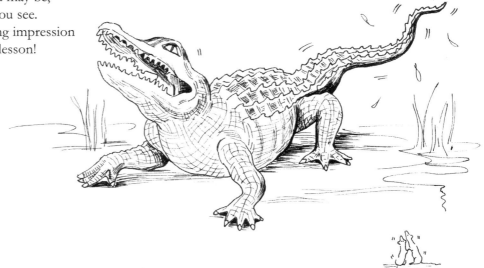

My floorboard-digging pig

What would you do? What would you do?
In the heat of the dusty day
If you saw my pig going dig dig dig
And ripping up your floorboards?

Would you go cuckoo and yell "Shoo! Shoo!"
As it excavated more boards?
If you saw my pig going dig dig dig
And ripping up your floorboards?

Would you shake your head and go to bed
- Could you really just ignore boards?
If you saw my pig going dig dig dig
And ripping up your floorboards?

Would you jump about and scream and shout
"Oh Gosh! Oh Crumbs! Oh Lor-boards!"
If you saw my pig going dig dig dig
And ripping up your floorboards?

Would you stay quite calm without alarm,
Say "It's only gently trying to gnaw boards"?
If you saw my pig going dig dig dig
And ripping up your floorboards?

No! I'd jump on its back
Give a mighty thwack
And roughly ride it doorwards!
If I saw your pig
Going dig dig dig
And ripping up
My floorboards!

Pets Are Pests

All pets are pests,
Says my mum, who detests
All the mess that they make
And the time that they take.

"As soon as it wakes up
The kitten wants food
Or maybe a stroke;
The hamster's made nests
In the J-cloths and jumpers -
It's really no joke.
What's that cat doing there?
It's really not fair -
That's your dad's favourite chair
And it's covered in hairs!
Now the dog wants a walk
So there's no time to talk
Before finding the lead,
And make sure you feed
The hamster and mice
And clean out the cages.
That smell isn't nice
And I've been telling you clearly
For ages and ages:
Looking after them's your task!

You said it was fun,
I'm not going to ask
You again: get it done!
And if the dog makes a mess
And the hamster a nest
In the T-shirts and vests
And the kitten goes missing
Then you'll understand - Yes!
That pets are all pests!"

Right! I've scrubbed and I've cleaned
And I've fed and I've walked
And I don't quite agree

                          ....but....
I'm starting to see what she means!

Flea facts

A flea can fly
As high as high as the sky
Or at least as high
As an aardvark's eye

If we could jump
Just like the flea
We could leap over houses
And coconut trees

But as fleas have needs
That are less than nice
Who'd be a flea?
We'd rather be mice!

flea

Cat / Fish

I'm a catfish, a catfish;
I'm really not a flatfish;
More a thisfish than a thatfish,
Not a thinfish, more a fatfish,
Not a mousefish, nor a ratfish.
I'm a capfish, not a hatfish
And if I have a fishwish,
It's a dogfish on a dish-wish!

Teacher's Hound

If I was a frog,
I'd hop
Out of the chair
And some people
Would scream!

If I was a jellyfish,
I'd flop
On the floor
Ane when someone trod on me
They'd slide across the room
And land with a clump
On their backside.

If I was an albatross,
I'd flap my wings
And look knowingly
As people fled outside.

If I was a seal,
I'd clap my flippers
And look shiny, cute and cool
As people smiled and wished
They could have a miniature one of me
In their fishpond or paddling pool.

But as I'm a hound,
The most patient animal
Ever to hop or bound
Flap or spring
Across the face of the earth
I'll just sit here waiting
For the hometime bell to ring.

The Dark Avenger

My dog is called The Dark Avenger
Hello, I'm Cuddles

She understands every word I say
Woof?

Last night I took her for a walk
Woof! Walkies! Let's go!

Cleverly, she kept 3 paces ahead
I dragged him along behind me

She paused at every danger, spying out the land
I stopped at every lamp-post

When the coast was clear, she sped on
I slipped my lead and ran away

Scenting danger, Avenger investigated
I found some fresh chip papers in the bushes

I followed, every sense alert
He blundered through the trees, shouting "Oy, Come 'ere! Where are you?"

Something - maybe a sixth sense - told me to stop
He tripped over me in the dark

There was a pale menacing figure ahead of us
Then I saw the white Scottie from next door

Avenger sprang into battle, eager to defend his master
Never could stand terriers

They fought like tigers
We scrapped like dogs

Until the enemy was defeated
Till Scottie's owner pulled him off - spoil sport!

Avenger gave a victory salute
I rolled in the puddles

And came to check I was all right
I shook mud over him

"Stop it, you stupid dog!"
He congratulated me

Sometimes, even The Dark Avenger can go too far.
Woof!! Yelp…!

Watch it!

Listen to me!
Yeah - me.
I know I'm small.
All right, I'm tiny
But I'm strong.
I've got special powers,
Extraordinary, scary powers
And I'm warning you
Don't mess with me.
Don't laugh.
Don't snigger.
Don't sneer.
Don't bring that cat
Anywhere near.
I won't tell you again.
I'm giving you
One last chance.
All right
You asked for it
!!NIP!!
I told you
Don't mess with
SUPERSHREW!!

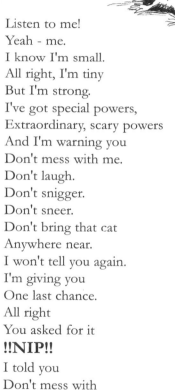

T Rex is coming to play!

Grrr… Graggghhh!!
Out of my way!
T Rex is coming to play!
Kept in the caverns
Like a toy in the drawer
Once a millennium
I come out and roar.
Shake the dust and the rust
Off my black scales
As I move like a train
That's come off the rails.
I strangle the dogs
Bite the heads off the sheep
Leave all the bones
In an untidy heap.
Keep out of my path
If you want to survive
For once a millennium
T Rex is alive!

Hark, sharks

Being a father
Is a responsible role
When you're a shark
At the head of the shoal.

You've got to teach 'em
And bring 'em up right:
Teach when to circle
And when to bite.

Sometimes be gentle
Sometimes be strict
Teach them how
That tail is flicked.

Look at me, children,
See my unblinking stare
Look how I keep
That fin in the air.

Oh yes, you have to teach 'em
And bring 'em up right,
So they know when to circle
And they know when to bite!

The impressionist mouse!
Fact: mice are well known mimics

I can bark like a shark
Moo like a shrew
I bet that's more
Than you can do.

I can meow like a cow
Neigh like a jay
I can be more things
Than you can say.

I can cluck like a duck
Bleat like a parakeet
Make lots of sounds
You couldn't repeat.

Mooing and barking all round the house,
Bleating and clucking:
I'm the impressionist mouse!

A Stegosaurus is for life

Down in a fern-decked valley
Far from the sun's fierce glare
A smiling stegosaurus
Laid her eggs with loving care.

But so as to protect them
From Tyrannosaurus Rex
She thought, "I'll dig a little hole
And cover up these eggs."

The soil around was rich and moist,
The hole she dug was deep.
The fine pink eggs they huddled there
As if they were asleep

Now Mrs Steg was charming
And kind to all she met
But she had one tiny little fault:
She was likely to forget.

So time went by and seasons passed,
An ice age came and went.
The eggs lay frozen in the earth
Near Tenterden in Kent.

One day a yellow JCB,
Laying pipelines for some gas,
Dug up five strange pink objects
And laid them in the grass.

Tim, Tam and Teddy saw them.
They took them home as toys

And in the middle of the night
They heard a tapping noise.

At first a claw crept through the crack,
Fast followed by a snout,
A head and then a body
As a grey-green ... thing ... hatched out!

The children were delighted.
They took them out for walks;
They fed them on bananas
And dandelion stalks.

The children grew up slowly:
The stegasauri grew up fast.
Their tails all sprouted deadly spikes
And their bony plates were vast.

"They'll have to go!" said grown ups
To science lab or zoo;
It might be to a circus -
We'll leave it up to you."

So

WANTED
Good home for some reptiles
As watchdogs they're the best
They'll babysit for hours
And stamp out household pests
Make all your neighbours jealous
Of your rockery on legs
They'll scare a burglar silly
And maybe lay you eggs!

One Worm Working

I hear one work working
One worm working in the ground

I hear two lions lying
Two lovely lions lying down
And one worm working in the ground

I hear three monkeys making...
Three monkeys making wishes
Two lovely lions lying down
And one worm working in the ground

I hear four froggies frying
Four froggies frying fishes
Three monkeys making wishes
Two lovely lions lying down
And one worm working in the ground

I hear five bees buzzing
Five bees buzzing in the air
Four froggies frying fishes
Three monkeys making wishes
Two lovely lions lying down
And one worm working in the ground

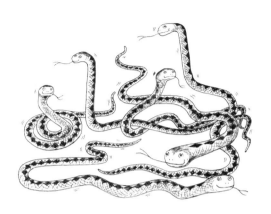

I hear six snakes hissing
Six snakes hissing over there
Five bees buzzing in the air
Four froggies frying fishes
Three monkeys making wishes
Two lovely lions lying down
And one worm working in the ground

I hear seven songbirds singing
Seven songbirds singing in the trees
Six snakes hissing over there
Five bees buzzing in the air
Four froggies frying fishes
Three monkeys making wishes
Two lovely lions lying down
And one worm working in the ground

I hear eight cats kissing
Eight cats kissing on my knees
Seven songbirds singing in the trees
Six snakes hissing over there
Five bees buzzing in the air
Four froggies frying fishes
Three monkeys making wishes
Two lovely lions lying down
And one worm working in the ground.

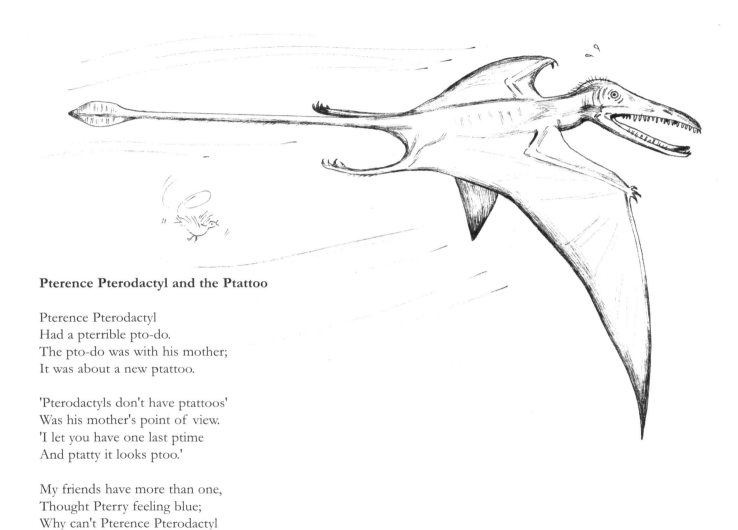

Pterence Pterodactyl and the Ptattoo

Pterence Pterodactyl
Had a pterrible pto-do.
The pto-do was with his mother;
It was about a new ptattoo.

'Pterodactyls don't have ptattoos'
Was his mother's point of view.
'I let you have one last ptime
And ptatty it looks ptoo.'

My friends have more than one,
Thought Pterry feeling blue;
Why can't Pterence Pterodactyl
Ptry ptwo ptatty ptattoos ptoo?

I fly on the wind

I fly on the wind of autumn,
I travel with the leaves
Of sycamore and oak and ash.
I travel on the breeze.

I fly on the wind of autumn.
I go where the west wind blows.
When the golden leaves fall to earth,
I go where the best wind knows.

Leave me to float with the autumn breeze.
Leave me to fly with the wind.
The sky is alight with the colours of fire
and I fly on the breath of the wind.

Fishilliteracy

Haddock can't spell
And skate can't write
Goldfish are hopeless
At reading at night.
Dolphins get by
With a language of signs
And eels can't get letters
To stay on fishy lines.
Sharks get their tenses
All in a muddle
And cod find apostrophes
Make them befuddled.
Give herring a book
And it soon falls asleep:
You just don't find libraries
Down in the deep.

It's a shock
It's a scandal
What shall we do?
Should we start
A fish school?
I leave that up to you…

Look out for the Headcat

At Tomkins school for top class cats
There's 50 felines and 50 mats,
A line of bowls on the stony floor
And a Headcat who rules with an awful claw.

Pity the moggie who loses the mouse,
Who can't find the sunniest place in the house;
Pity the tom whose homework is late,
Who cannot sit still and patiently wait!

So, practise the meows, perfect the naps,
Learn the purrs for all kinds of laps,
Know how to stand and paw at the door
and look out for the Headcat with the awfulest claw!

A Pet in the Car

Before we set off
My dad said:
There's no room for that thing.
My mum said:
It's unhygienic.
My sister said:
Leave it at home.
But I said:
It'll be no trouble, and anyway, it's magic.

On the way
My dad said:
It's making a noise.
(It was only snuffling.)
My mum said:
Can't it keep it still?
(It was only shuffling.)
My sister said:
It smells.
But I said
Nothing.
Thinking,
They don't appreciate my magic pet.

Later
My dad said:
A puncture!
My mum said:
In the middle of nowhere!
My sister said:
I don't believe it!
And I said:
The spare is flat.

They all said:
What shall we do?
And I said:
I'll go for help!
And they said:
How?
And I said:
On my magic pet!

They looked disbelieving -
But I'm nearly there now,
Speeding along
On my magic car pet.

To Grandma's by Snake

We went for a trip with an anaconda.
It revved its engines and went for a wanda
Zipping through the trees on its jungle Honda.

We caught a ride on a boa constrictor.
She was long and slender and that's why we picked her -
Cos no tough terrain was gonna affect her!

We couldn't get a bus so we caught an adder.
We held on tight as it climbed up ladders
And dropped us off here feeling wiser and gladder...

"Did you have a good journey?" our Grandma cried.
"Serpently! Serpently!" we replied.

Reptile rap

There's someone in the forest
who's so reptilian!
Her tail is long
and her name is Gillian.
She's a creature
who's one in a million:
her scales are shiny
and her name is Gillian.
I love the way her eyes
are always open wide
and the way her tongue
darts from side to side;
I love her fangs;
don't care she's got no chin
and I love the way
she sloughs her skin!
I love the way she slides;
I love the way she slithers;
I love the way her wriggles
say 'Come hither…'
hold me in your coils
and never let me go
let me be, oh, let me be
your reptile Romeo!
Yeh - there's someone in the forest
who's so reptilian:
her tail is long
and her name is Gillian!

Croc Doc

Being a doctor to crocodiles isn't easy;
They feel sorry for themselves when their stomachs are queasy,
Their snouts are pale and their eyes are bleary
As they lie so low and say, "Doc, I'm so weary
And my tail is heavy like lead lined piping,
My nose is runny, needs constant wiping
With a handkerchief that's long and so thin -
Believe me, Doc, I've no strength to grin.
There's a pain in my tooth when I open wide
And no one will risk a look inside.
My head is aching and my breathing is wheezy..."
No, a croc doc's life is certainly not easy!

Hawk

from
nowhere
a dot
a cross
an arrow
pointing its path
the hawk
dark mark of death
hurtles to earth
brakes
takes
ascends
is gone
somewhere

The long-leg spider

I'm the long-leg spider
That's fallen in your bath
I'm the scary spider
That's standing in your path
    That's standing in your path

Don't wash me down the plug hole
Don't squash me with a shoe
I only prey on insects
I do no harm to you!

I'm just a little spider
That's fallen in your bath
Please drop me in the garden
Let me run off down the path
    Let me run off down the path!

Mole Song

I'm under the ground
Yes, I'm under the ground
I don't make a sound
As I'm pushing up a mound.

First there's a bump
Then there's a lump
Next thing you know
There's a great big hump.

I'm under the ground
Yes, I'm under the ground
I don't make a sound
As I'm pushing up a mound.

I've got a little pink nose
And eyes half-closed
Big strong legs
And tunnelling toes!

I'm under the ground
Yes, I'm under the ground
I don't make a sound
As I'm pushing up a mound.

Squirrel Song

I fall asleep in the winter
I wake up in the spring
I snore all through the winter
And in the summer I sing

I sing the quiet song of the squirrel
I sing about branches and trees
I sing where I hid my best acorns
I sing to the birds and the bees

Then I fall asleep in the winter
I wake up in the spring
I snore all through the winter
And in the summer I sing

Christmas Cat

The Christmas cat sits still and sleek,
The Christmas cat is wary,
She's been in trouble twice this week;
She's finding Christmas scary.

The Christmas cat tried to join in,
She played with Christmas lights.
She pulled the tree right off the stool
And gave them all a fright.

The Christmas cat likes Christmas food,
She likes the Christmas meat.
She likes to lick the turkey fat
And get between our feet.

The Christmas cat is shut outside:
She'd grabbed the Christmas fairy.
She's been in trouble twice this week;
She's finding Christmas SCARY!

Monster of the Deep

I'm a monster of the deep
And I really like to sleep
With my tentacles in a heap
In the deep.

I'm a monster of the deep
And I really like to creep
Like a wolf upon some sheep
In the deep.

I'm a monster of the deep
And I really like to keep…keeeep…keeeeeep
My arms around you till you weep
   Weeeep
         Weeeeeeep!
In the deep...

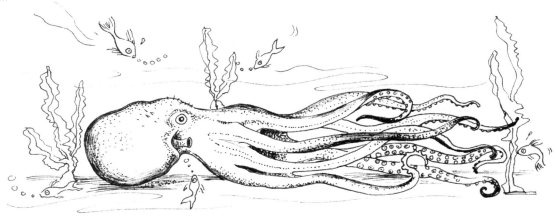

Croc's lament

A crocodile
Will rarely smile
She knows your plans are drastic

She will save her skin
With a mirthless grin
And suggest you use some plastic

The Ballad of Unicorn Isle

Make a wish when the geese are flying overhead and you may see the unicorns again.

Once upon a faraway time
Before the clocks had learned to chime
When every river spoke in rhyme
Once upon a time

Once within a distant land
Where mountains hadn't heard of man
Where dolphins played and bluebirds sang
Once within a land

Then and there in echoing light
Where gold was day and silver night
Lived unicorns of purest black and white
There in echoing light

One shining day in shimmering glade
The seer had come to speak they said
An ancient one with eyes of jade
One shimmering shining day

"I saw the future far away -
Hearken friends to what I say!
I saw grey night and I saw grey day
In the future far away!

I saw the pale two legged beast
Rise up from west, rise up from east
And slay our kind for fun and feast
The pale two-legged beast.

It hunted down the unicorn
It cut off head, it cut off horn
Or stole our foals as they were born
And caged the noble unicorn."

Once upon a desperate hour
In the shadow of the great moonflower
They made a pact to use their power
Upon a desperate hour.

So faded they from human sight
Though wild geese see them from their flight
And children dream of them at night
Invisible to human sight

Once within a faraway land
Where unicorns first heard of man
Where hotels rise and tourists tan
Once within a land...

The Ghost of Iguanadon

My name is iguanadon
And I stalk the world at night
I'm a ghostly kind of creature -
Yet no one gets a fright.
For I'm not seen by human eyes
And my footprints make no sound -
I just haunt the old stone valleys
Where the ancient bones are found.
You won't feel my feverish breath
You won't hear my dreadful roar
Cos I'm the ghost of iguanadon
The dinosaur that no one saw…